MW01595693

With love
and best wishes

[signature]

Be and it Is

and it

Volume I

Be *and it* Is

Volume I

INSPIRATIONS
OF
EMPOWERMENT

Amyn Dahya

British Cataloguing in Publication Data
Dahya, Amyn 1957-
Be and It Is
Volume 1

ISBN 1904428088

1. Self Development 2. Inspiration 3 Philosophy.

Production: Empowered Living Publications

First Printing December 2002
Second Printing September 2005

10987654321
Empowered Living Publications

Cover and Layout by
bioprana@teleline.es (Rafael Barea and Juan de Dios Crespo)
Printed by Eurocolor, S.A. (Madrid-Spain)

Dedication

This book is dedicated to all those who seek to enrich their lives by drawing upon the limitless potential that resides within.

May you open the appropriate pages each day to discover the inspirations that await you.

When you say, Be, it Is...

Table of Contents

Dedication	V
Team Work	2
Giving	4
Accomplishment	6
The Past	8
Workaholics	10
Ego	12
Sin	14
Regret	16
Courage	18
The Stars	20
Living	22
Achievement	24
Abundance	26
Universality of Religion	28
Struggle	30
Criticism	32
First Love	34
Motivation	36
Revenge	38
Laziness	40
Powers of Conflict	42
Fear	44
Wealth	46
Love	48

Inner Voice	50
Legacy	52
Competition	54
Essence	56
Destiny	58
Generosity	60
Creating Tomorrow	62
Detachment	64
Be Available	66
Humility	68
Siblings	70
An Exalted Destiny	72
Information	74
Beauty	76
Leader	78
The Eagle	80
Eliminating Conflict	82
The Impossible	84
Risk	86
Solitude	88
Failure	90
Children	92
Rain	94
Birthday	96
Homework	98
Mother	100
Now	102
Enterprise	104

For Children 106
Credit 108
Exploitation 110
Count your Blessings 112
The Present 114
Our Heroes 116
Bullying 118
Work 120
Power 122
Sadness 124
Wisdom 126
Conflict 128
Essence of Humanity 130
Respecting Food 132
Death 134
True Power 136
Results 138
A Bright Future 140
Respect 142
Rejection 144
Father 146
The Power of the Present 148
Friends 150
Precious Blessings 152
Steel 154
The Contest 156
Ponder 158
Two Face 160

Life	162
Patience	164
Laws of Science	166
Honesty	168
A Peaceful World	170
Respecting Life	172
Letting Go	174
Building Fences	176
The Key to Happiness	178
Enlightenment	180
Happiness	182
Solving Problems	184
The Law of the Eternal Pool	186
Authority	188
Freedom	190
Little Things	192
Blame	194
Unity	196
Determination	198
In Love	200
Disappointments	202
Marriage	204

Be

and it **Is**

Volume I

❧ Teamwork

When all the rays come together
They form the sun

Teamwork brings power... ❧

❧ Giving

When a tree gives us its fruit
It expects nothing in return

When the Sun brings us
Light and warmth
It expects nothing in return

When water quenches
Our burning thirst
It expects nothing in return

Why then can we not
Give freely of ourselves

Without expecting something in return?

Give freely... ❧

✥ *Accomplishment*

If dawn is the start of life
Which stands on pillars of trust

Then dusk is the end of life
That must stand on pillars of
accomplishment

Achieve all you can today... ❧

✌§ The Past

The past is a barometer
That helps guide the future

Learn from the past... ৡ

❧ Workaholics

Your body and its energy
Are like a bank

When you borrow
You must replace

Take a break... ❧

✒ *Ego*

Ego is like short eyesight
That does not see beyond itself

For out there lies
A world of abundance

Whose doors are seldom crossed
By the short sighted

Abandon your ego... ❧

✑§ *Sin*

A sin is committed
When we fail to recognise
That the playground of life
Has rules

Think before you act... ❧

✍ Regret

Regret is a great teacher
If one seeks meaning
From one's mistakes

Reflect on your mistakes... ❧

❧ Courage

Courage is like a fire
That burns with
Strength and freedom

Warming the heart
And illuminating the soul

Extinguishing forever
The darkness of fear

Be bold... ❧

❧ The Stars

The stars are not balls of fire
In the sky

They are aspects of knowledge
In the universe

*There is more to everything
than meets the eye...* ❧

✎§ *Living*

Each day is a life in itself
At sunrise we are born
And at sunset we die

Life is indeed a sum
Of many thousand births
And deaths

Live each day to its fullest
As if it were your last

Get your priorities right... ❧

❧ *Achievement*

We do not need
To reach out for the stars
If we can bring them to us

We can achieve the unachievable
With our feet firmly planted
On the ground

Achieve with wisdom... ❧

⊷§ *Abundance*

Abundance lies in having one
Abundance lies in having all

Numbers bear no meaning
For unity can never be measured
And raindrops can never be counted

The greatest abundance lies
In being one with yourself

Be rich, love yourself... ❧

✌ः *Universality of Religion*

Look into the Message
Behind each religion

After removing the clouds
Of rituals and traditions

You will discover
That all religions are equal

For they carry the same universal
Message

Live in harmony... ❧

✌❧ *Struggle*

Struggle is a step
In the staircase of life

Climb it with strength... ❧

◆§ *Criticism*

Criticism is the language
Of the imperfect

Who live within the illusion
Of perfection

Do not criticise... ❧

≈§ *First Love*

Every seed is kissed with life
By its first droplet of water

O beloved first love
You brought life to my love
You brought warmth to my soul

Countless winters have gone by
Freezing time into the ice

Countless flowers have blossomed
In the springs that brought freedom
To my unfolding life

No matter where the years may have
come or gone

There always glows the flame in my
heart
That you so tenderly lit

Bless you... ❧

✑ *Motivation*

Motivation is like the heartbeat
When it stops, we die

Live forever, be motivated... ❧

✺ Revenge

Revenge is a fire
That only burns its beholder

Forgive and forget... ❧

⪼ Laziness

The tortoise plods slowly on its path
The hare races through the forest
The eagle soars in the skies

Each one on a journey of its own
Whose time is so well appointed

The one who wastes time
By postponing today for tomorrow
Walks along a path
That leads to nowhere

Do not waste time... ❧

❧ *Powers of Conflict*

Conflict can be powerful
For it spreads quickly
Given the right fuel

Conflict can be powerless
For it can be eliminated
By simple thought and consciousness

Conflict is a state of mind... ❧

❧ Fear

Fear comes from our inability
To embrace the unknown

Accept the unknown... ❧

❧ Wealth

Wealth is like an ocean
We can all drink from it
And its level will never fall

Do not try to put the ocean
In your pocket

For you will surely drown

Beware of greed... ❧

✑Love

Love is neither an emotion
Nor is it a feeling

Love is a reality that brings together
One, two and all

Be in love, always... ❧

Inner Voice

Always listen to your inner voice

If a relationship or transaction
Does not feel right
Do not do it

Listen to yourself... ð

❧ Legacy

Give your children
The best part of you

For through them
You may live forever

Build your legacy wisely... ❧

❧ Competition

Competition is an energy
That cuts like a sword
With two edges on its shining blade

The blunt one is a tool that creates
And the sharp one
A weapon that destroys

Hold the sword
In your hand each day
And watch with the eyes of a hawk
The blade that you bring forth

For the joy of creation
And the pain of destruction
Are yours to be experienced

Compete with fairness... ❧

◈§ Essence

Essence is the unseen element
Which gives life and character
To the form

Essence is the soul
Whose presence is felt and known
In what we see
And what we don't

Seek essence... ॐ

❧ Destiny

Destiny is neither created
Nor ordained

It is an experience of the continuous
That has no beginning
And no end

Experience every moment... ❧

✍§ Generosity

You expect life to grant
Your birthright each day

Of the rays of the warm sun
Of the water from the blessed earth
Of air from the limitless skies
Of sustenance from nature's best
Of love from the mate of your soul
Of wisdom from the universe
Of success on a path you know not
Of all the bounties that you pray for
Now and forever

How then can you deny
Those whom you encounter
The birthright that they have travelled
so far to receive

Give freely of that which you cherish
For that is your birthright
Of ultimate fulfilment

Be generous... ❦

❧ Creating Tomorrow

*When we harness the present
We create the future*

Seize the moment... ❧

≈§ Detachment

Detachment brings freedom
That allows us to flow like water
Towards the fulfilment of our goals

Do not cling too tightly... ॐ

✌§ Be Available

Time is scarce
For it has always been so

For the stone-age men
Who chased deer
To the busybodies of today
Pursuing material plenty

Important as you believe
Your time may be
Do not make yourself
Scarce to others

For while water
Is scarce in the desert
It manifests into an oasis
Bearing life and quenching thirst
Of the countless
Who walk the burning sands

Carving a path that leads forever
To its blessed source
Available to all

Be the oasis, not the desert... ❧

Humility

One who has seen the earth
From the stars

Knows how the greatest
Lives within the smallest

Be humble... ❧

✒ Siblings

Every fruit in an orchard
Is endowed with seeds
That stick together
As their world ripens

Sharing love, strength and unity
That lives forever
Beyond the harvest

Love your siblings... ❧

❧ An Exalted Destiny

A life that is led by decisions
Drawn from inner wisdom
Is no ordinary destiny

It is an exalted destiny

Make inspired decisions... ❧

❧ Information

Information is a meal
That is received with gratitude
Savoured with joy
Digested in time
And returned once again
To the soil it came from

Share information... ❦

❧ Beauty

Every being is endowed with a face
Some beautiful
Some not

The difference lies not in its features
But in the happiness that it radiates

Be happy, be beautiful... ❧

⊷ *Leader*

A leader always belongs
In a league of his own

He is different from everyone

It is indeed this difference
That causes others to follow him

Be unique and original... ❧

ঙ The Eagle

A single flap of the eagle's wings
Takes it through a great distance
At a speed
That all birds could only envy

Live life like the eagle
Fly through your challenges
With maximum speed
And minimum effort

Be smart... ❧

✑ Eliminating Conflict

Conflict can be killed
Simply by the way people think
Either individually or as a group

Be free of conflict... ❧

❧ The Impossible

We live in a world
Of infinite possibilities

How can there exist
Something so rare
As the impossible

Everything is possible... ❧

✌ *Risk*

Risk is an adventure
For the foolish and the wise
Venturing into the ocean of life
To claim their waves

One discovers the crests
And one the troughs
But discover they do
For life is a journey of discovery

Yet, out there lie those
Who risk nothing
Shrivelling in the desert
As they foolishly chase
The sand dunes
Believing they are waves

Do not be afraid to take risks... ও~

❧ Solitude

There is no such thing as solitude
For when you are with yourself
You are with everything

You are never alone... ❧

❧ Failure

*Failure is a blessing
That paves the way for success*

Do not lament... ❦

◈ Children

*Our children do not belong to us
We are simply their custodians for a
short period of time*

Do your best for them... ❧

❧ Rain

Rain is a blessing
Not a curse

Rain never ruins a day
For it creates the day

Rain brings life
A life of hope

For behind every dark rain cloud
Lies the sun

Waiting to shine upon you

Be happy in sunshine and rain... ❧

∞§ Birthday

Every day of your life is a birthday
To celebrate
To reflect upon
And to understand
That life's journey
Limited as it seems
Is the greatest of steps
In the voyage of the soul
That is limitless and pure

Celebrate every day... ❧

❧ Homework

Homework is the dessert
That completes the great meal of
learning

Treat it with importance... ॐ

❧ Mother

A mother is the ocean
That cradles your soul
Protecting you from rain and snow

As you tenderly grow
Amidst her waves of love
Nurturing you gently to her shores

So that you may flow
On your journey
And ascend your destiny
From river to cloud

As she awaits with open arms
The rainfall of life
To shower upon her
The precious droplet
In whom she lives forever

Love your mother... ❧

≈ Now

When you write now backwards
It reads won

Harness now
And all will be won

Be a winner... ❧

✒ Enterprise

Do not be afraid to take risks
For nothing ventured
Is nothing gained

If you do not cast your line
In the water
You will never catch the fish
That is for sure

Be enterprising... ❧

❧ For Children

Life is like a quick snapshot
Take the right picture
For this is your chance

Do your best... ❧

❧ Credit

One who claims credit for the work of others

Discovers an overdraft
In all life's endeavours

Give credit where it is due... ❧

✑ Exploitation

The earth was created
With perfect order
Like a jigsaw puzzle
Whose pieces
Found their resting place
With ease and grace

Then came the human being
Endowed with a perfect form
Within which dwelt
An imperfect mind
Whose only order was disorder

The blessed earth laments today
For no pieces of the jigsaw puzzle
Can ever find their place again
As they lie in captivity
In the pockets of their greedy masters

Harness the resources of nature
with respect... ࣸ

✎§ Count your Blessings

Learn to count
The blessings that you have
For they are truly yours

And don't grieve
For what you do not have
For it was never yours

Appreciate what you have... ❧

✌ **The Present**

The past is a memory
And the future is an expectation

The only reality that exists
is in the present

Live in the present... ❧

➳§ Our Heroes

We raise our hands
To salute the great ones
Who gave their life
To defend our cause

If only we could see our heroes
Looking back at us
With wisdom in their eyes

Asking why

War is never the answer... ❧

❧ Bullying

A bully is like a dry well
That threatens to get you wet

Do not fear bullies... ❧

✑ Work

Work is a blessing that brings us self-worth

*Respect your work
If you value yourself*

Take pride in your work... ❧

✑ *Power*

Power is an illusion
For it doesn't exist

When you exercise power upon others
You become the illusion itself

When you empower others
You become reality itself

Choose reality... ❦

✑ *Sadness*

Sadness is a fruit from the tree of life
A fruit that brings
The taste of experience

There is no such thing
As a good experience
And there is no such thing
As a bad experience

For life itself is experience

Make the most of every experience... ❧

✒ Wisdom

Wisdom comes from knowing the difference
Between fire and ice

Dwelling in fire brings lessons
Of the joys of light
And the pains of heat

Embracing ice brings knowledge
Of frost and chills
Cradled amidst stillness and peace

Only when one has traversed the earth
From the lava in its belly
To its frozen poles
Can one recognise wisdom

As it shines from the unseen
To give birth to immortal decisions

Respect wisdom... ❧

❧ Conflict

Conflict is like a virus
It breeds, multiplies and spreads
Infecting all those that come in its way

Avoid conflict... ❧

❧ Essence of Humanity

We are all woven together
As one humanity through essence

From where shines
Love, understanding and forgiveness
That we owe to one another

Love thy neighbour... ❧

☙ Respecting Food

It is said in the Book of the Universe
That each grain in this world
Has the name of he or she
Who is to feed from it

Respect your food, for it has found you... ৡঌ

✁ Death

Death is a continuation
Of that which was interrupted by birth

Life in this world
Is but a short stop
In the passage of eternity

Celebrate life, do not grieve... ❧

✑ True Power

In the centre of the cyclone
Lies complete stillness

Live within it, not around it... ❧

❧ Results

Results are a simple measure
Of things we endeavour

Guiding us like a compass
Towards success and fulfilment

Experienced only by those
Who focus on the measure
Rather than its reward

Results are stepping stones, not destinations... ঽ৵

✎§ A Bright Future

Never before in history
Has every human being
Possessed so much inner power
To change the future of this planet
For the better

Make this world a better place... ❧

✒ *Respect*

Respect cannot be bought
Neither can it be sold

Respect can only be earned
At a price that all can afford

Respect everyone... ❧

❧ Rejection

Rejection is a pain
That comes from not knowing
That all the love that could ever exist
Lies within you

You are above rejection... ❧

✍ Father

A father is the tree
Whose shade protects you from the sun
And cools you in the heat

The trunk of this blessed tree
Carries you rung by rung
Up the ladder of life
So that you may touch the skies
And taste the heavens

Love your father... ❧

❧ The Power of the Present

It is only in the present
That we can explore, realise,
embrace and harness
The pure energy that we are

Experience now.... ❧

✒ Friends

Friends are not just people
They are souls who share in your life's
journey

Cherish your friends... ❦

◄§ *Precious Blessings*

We never stop to recognise
Life's most precious blessings

For we are too busy
Being the centres of our own little
universes

Cherish your loved ones... ❧

❧ Steel

Steel is cold
Steel is hard
Steel is not as strong as it seems

For it can be bent
By a ray of warmth
From a heart filled with love
And from words filled with kindness

Be warm, always
It is not cool to be cold... ❧

❧ The Contest

If you make life a contest
Between victory and defeat
You will feel highs
And suffer lows

Be neutral... ৡৡ

~§ Ponder

Live your life each day
As if it were your last

Then ask yourself
How you feel about worldly success
or failure

Focus on that which is truly important... ❧

✑ Two Faces

One who is two faced
Cannot look into a mirror
For there will be a stranger
Looking back

Be frank and honest... ع‌

◦§ Life

Life is a series of crossroads
At each crossroad
We make our choice
To turn left or right
Or go straight ahead

The choice we make
Determines what crossroad we will
face next

Choose wisely... ❧

◆§ Patience

The tree stands tall in its own time
With its roots
Firmly anchored into the earth
And its trunk
Endowed with strength
To withstand a thousand storms

The rosebud blossoms in its own time
Revealing a flower
Whose colour and scent
Are of the divine

A child is born, in its own time
Bringing laughter and joy
To its newly discovered world

All things perfect
Manifest in their own time

Why then do you rush through life
O dear friend
For it is your greatest gift of all
To be unwrapped with patience
In its own time

Be patient... ❧

✒ Laws of Science

In science, there can be no laws
For if an explorer followed laws
His or her discovery would be limited
To the boundaries of such laws

Think broader... ❧

❧ *Honesty*

Honesty is neither a strength
Nor a virtue

For it is born from truth
Whose power is beyond measure

Seek truth... ঌ

❧ A Peaceful World

We must learn to resolve conflict
By reasoning rather than war

Reasoning that is driven
By ethics and spiritual balance
Discards confrontation at its source

Make peace, not war... ও

✧§ Respecting Life

Only one who has the power to give life

Has the right to take life

Do not kill... ❧

✑ Letting Go

If you truly love something
You must be able to set it free

If it comes back to you
It is truly yours

If not
It never was

Give freedom, let go... ❧

✒ Building Fences

The moment we build a fence around us

We begin to shrink from within
and beyond

The more fences we build
The quicker we will disappear

Be open and share... ❧

❧ The Key to Happiness

Learn to let it be

Do not force
Events and circumstances
To meet your desires

For that will make you unhappy

Let your desires follow the events
For therein lies happiness

Let it be... ❧

✑ Enlightenment

You do not have to deny yourself
The gifts that life brings
To find enlightenment

For that which you seek
Resides within you
Who then are you really denying?

Enjoy life, with balance... ❧

✣ Happiness

Happiness is like a chameleon
That takes the colour of its beholder

While all colours of the rainbow
Can never be the same

Seek happiness each day
No matter what colours life brings to you

Happiness has many dimensions
Recognise them... ❧

❧ Solving Problems

The most complex of problems
Have the simplest of solutions

Seek the simple answers first... ❧

✍ The Law of the Eternal Pool

The Eternal Pool
Provides all the resources of life
From health to wealth
To wisdom and more

Its law is simple to follow
For that which comes must also go
To maintain it's blessed flow

Generosity is a two-way street
For resources only flow
Through open hands
One that gives
And one that receives

Discover abundance through giving... ❧

✍ *Authority*

One who has true authority
Never needs to exercise it

Be humble... ೫

✺❧ *Freedom*

Freedom is not something we give
Neither is it something we can ever
take

Freedom is a state of being
That flourishes in the hearts of all

Respect freedom... ❧

✒ *Little things*

Little things in life
Often carry a large meaning

We fail to recognise this simple truth
Amidst our little self-centred worlds

Be observant... ❧

❧ Blame

A finger that is pointed in blame
Is like an arrow
That pierces the heart

Causing a wound
That grows each day
Giving birth to new arrows
That will one day
Discover their target

Do not blame... ❧

◆§ Unity

Unity is not a number that you
can count

For when you are in unity
You are everything

Be united... ঌ

✌ Determination

*Determination sows seeds
of possibility in the impossible*

Be determined... ❧

✍§ *In love*

Allowing the mind to make decisions
for the heart
Is like using a ten foot metal pole
Instead of a paintbrush
To produce a painting

Follow your heart... ❧

৺ *Disappointments*

There can be no disappointments in life
If you do not cling to your expectations

Let it be... ❧

❧ Marriage

Marriage is not a partnership
Nor is it a contract

Marriage is a union
That binds two blessed rays
With the sun itself

Be One... ❧

About the Author

Amyn Dahya is an internationally acclaimed scientist, author and spiritual healer, who produces works of inspiration in the form of parables and insights, that articulate complex concepts about our material and spiritual lives, in a simple form that can be understood by people of all ages, cultures and walks of life.

He travels extensively around the world, sharing his inspirations in the form of books, lectures, seminars and workshops. He also helps people to heal themselves through meditation, by teaching them to tap into their inner

reservoir of creative and healing
energies. To date, he has helped
thousands of people on a voluntary, no
charge basis, to heal themselves from
physical, mental and emotional
ailments ranging from terminal cancer
to depression.

Amyn Dahya's writings foster a special
bond between the reader and his or her
inner self, thus creating an
understanding of the message that is
being conveyed, at a deep, personal
level. This has been the experience of
readers of his books all over the world.

Books and Lectures

Books

Reflections from the Origin
ISBN 0-9682683-1-5

Parables from the Origin
ISBN 0-9682683-2-3

¡Sea! y asi Será
ISBN 1904428096

Towards Zero Conflict
ISBN 1904428118

Lectures (Audio Tapes & CD's)

Meditation I - Alignment of the Body and
Intellect ISBN 1904428010

Meditation II - The Spiritual Journey
ISBN 1904428002

Exploring Limitless Horizons
ISBN 1-9044281-3-4

Empowered Living Foundation

Website:
www.amyndahya.com

Email:
info@amyndahya.com